Love Poems

Between your Beloved Heart beat and the plane
of this book is simply a line going for a short journey
between the vital fragrance of passion and poetry to
The Temple Of LOVE , where the Elysian Field kisses
Your Beloved Soul with the blanket of tenderness
to open Your Wings Of LOVE to give this
Universe all its allure, beauty and elegance
As LOVE is a sublime Divine limpid mirror
that reflects your Heart's purity.

Love Poems

This book is gratefully dedicated to the World of all Lovers,
Where the fragility of LOVE has passionate fevers to
receive the royalty of Hearts, where the Beloved LOVE is
sublime riddle wrapped in tenderness with the kiss of
inextinguishable flame of begotten LOVE Story.
And to Mona, my Beloved Wife; my fervent solemn passion,
The Temple Of Devotion, and to Emilia and Ethan;
Adoring twins,The basket of kisses, my Beloved children,
The ebullient Phantom Of LOVE, my Beloveds fortress of life,
And to my Beloved Parents;
My Loving paradise of serenity, The Temple Of Tenderness,
And to ADONAI ; The Holy One , Blessed be He;
"The Ultimate Poem",
The Supreme Beloved Embodiment Of Eternal LOVE.

Table of Contents

My LOVE 6
Your Devoted Loving Hands 11
The Sea Of LOVE 16
My Longing Tears 21
Mother 25
LOVE Vows 30
The Season Of LOVE 35
Love Touched Me 37
The Blanket Of LOVE 39
Forgiveness 44
Your Loving touch 46
The Attainment 48
LOVE enfolds forgiveness 50
Vanished into LOVE 54
Open thine own Heart 57
The Sunrise of LOVE 60
Heart 64
The Infinite 67
Inception Of LOVE 72
Secret Place 78
The Anatomy Of Heart 83
Loving Souls 90
Jerusalem 96
The Prayers 104
FACE OF LOVE 107

Love Poems

My LOVE

My Beloved,
My fervent Solemn passion,
My LOVE bound to you
My Darling, I am entirely thine
As kindling in pure Formidable flame
My Beloved, My precious love
My better self,
If the moment of Immortality
Unveil to exist between us
I shalt whisper your Beloved name
As phantom of delight
Riveting as melodious
As mating birds

My Beloved,
My fervent Solemn passion,
Your elegance and beauty
As begotten rapturous vibrant
ebullient portrait of LOVE
As blissful birth of precious

glittering mother of pearl
Invigorating to purify
my tumultuous untamed heart

My Immortal Angel,
My Dearest LOVE
My Joyful Darling
My eyes, worships Your Eyes
In pure adoration
My eyes can NO longer
hide my addiction

My Immortal Beloved
The LOVE of sublimity,
Should I not let my eyes
become lit, before YOUR eyes
As my heart's pupil of febrile eyes
Dives in your endless ocean
of LOVE to be drowned in ecstasy

My Beloved,
My fervent Solemn passion,
My hunger has become a fain of fasting
My Darling,
Your Lips, a provocative budding beauty
which Loves to flaunts itself
shalt be my eternal
Adoring site of pilgrimage,
As my tender lips, as nourishing
As endless waves of ocean
can not resist rushing to wet
to rescue YOUR thirst of ecstasy

My Beloved,
My fervent Solemn passion,
Faithfullest heart,
My Love bound to you, As we stem
As rose garden of Elysium
As sweet scent of LOVE
Emanating from the blossoms
As our tender hands entangled
with Majestic Red Robe Of LOVE
As Our eyes wed
For moment of eternal serenity
to cast our Hearts net in endless
ocean of sublime ecstasy
to capture our own image of ONENESS

My Immortal Beloved
Sanctuary of Love, My Darling,
I am entirely Thine,
I clasp the hand of Love
As I clasp my body
As fortitude of Love
Against YOUR body,
The Citadel of Heaven,
As my lips penetrates the silence
to whisper tenderly in Thy Beloved ears;
I LOVE THEE,
As My hearts infinite tender majesty
Shalt illuminate the Devine promise of bliss
As it echoes in eternity,
As my heart decorate the tent of LOVE

My Beloved, My fervent
My Solemn passion,
My Darling, My precious one,
My soul exclaimed in delight jublation
My Beloved LOVE
As I am fain to see THEE
in the Bethel of LOVE,
For Eternity
Forever Thine
Forever Ours

Your Devoted Loving Hands

Your devoted adoring Loving hands
Shields the abyss with trance
in utter bewilderment
As every hand is first an apprentice
That slaves beneath The Temple Of LOVE

Your Loving hands have valor and daring
to weave my sorrow into a sublime
blanket of LOVE and tenderness
Your Loving hands touching my face
As a twin gentle rivulets, to the ballad it sings
Like murmuring limpid charming reveries
of past sweet remembrances
With adoring bassinets of kisses
As crimson lips,
faithful, gaiety and felicitous
As riveting colorful tender roses
Sensual, aromatic, suffused with happiness
Utterly rattling my soul as it engraves
the headstone of the begotten LOVE poems

My heart turned to effulgent roses
it keeps opening , as the fragile glass
door of my heart becomes very capricious
inviting my LOVE to eternally dance in bliss
under The Temple of your Loving hands

Your glimmering adoring hands
As rise of sun upon awe-inspiring morning
As an inscrutable countenance of tenderness
As the inception of life's journey, melts in bliss
ends with thee, enraptured by your melodies

And now, unwittingly
You've made me a LOVE Story
A LOVE song of violets dream
and my soul's forgotten gleam
longing for you, breathlessly
indeed, you are the sacred holy
secret of Lover's hidden sanctuary

No devote of gentle LOVE
Ever display ostentatiously
Every whim of the Beloved
As I worship your Loving hands
A maven of never ending kindness
I adore you, I worship you for eternity
in a merciful mirage, in a manner
most graven, as my every reason of being
gazing at your Loving hands
perplexedly mesmerized by
glittering romance of your heart

Thy Loving hands,
an opulence tender majesty
an intimate treasure to surmise
I trust in thy Loving hands
They touch my heart so deeply
to bloom and shelter the
shadow of my LOVE,
as abiding, faithful, Loving companion

Thou art mine champion of excellence
a lovely temperance of courageous
inner strength and puissance
with equal grace, elegance and aplomb
utterly, a boundless queen of royalty
crowned with gentleness and indulgence

Thy adoring praising hands,
The Temple Of Devotion
Tucked under the wings of my LOVE
A pilgrimage site sanctuary to refugee
of fears wielded by the sword of tenderness

As my impotent wisdom hath bowed
In utmost respect to thy righteousness
Innocence and purity
How I admire the gallantry of thy spirit
as unlocking key of wisdom
to the stairway of tenderness
as a serene journey
upon majestic mount of Elysium
Thy presence is the blossom of my heart
I shalt recall thy gratitude

As I am still yours, as I wast owned by Thou
As thy Loving hands
As circumference of bliss
As a firmament accompanying a star
As I am yours,
Forever thine

The Sea Of LOVE

My LOVE Is pulsating with devotion
Like an epistemic wave on stormy ocean,
The captain of my heart steered our LOVE
Through a raging tempest venture
amid supernal beacons of delight,
Secretly aspired to transpire the droplet
Of rivulets drifting in the serenity of LOVE

In the Sea of LOVE my flame of passion
devour the winds of the Vessel of our hearts
In the Sea of LOVE,
the waves of Your Beloved Heart rate
Caressing the sands of my LOVE
As if the Fairy has sprinkle her loving
blanket of tenderness along the glistening
golden seashores of my longing yearning

Come to My seashore of LOVE
Where you are as the infinite Sea of LOVE
and my LOVE NOTES are the grains

of sands upon the shores of devotions
Come to My seashore of LOVE
to see the handprint Of MY SOUL
Carved with an adoring happy tidings
Of, I LOVE YOU,
Engraved with the blood of my heart

Let us Leave this World of Ignorance
As the Pearl of Our LOVE
Is The Temple Of LOVERS
Built by devotion around the Grains of Sand
As the sun kissed endless ocean of LOVE
Embraces Your pearly sheen HEART with devotion
Where your Beloved Heart is the Infinite
Sea Of LOVE and its every Heart beat
Is an adoring LOVE Note in every drop of its water
Fear NO fate, MY LOVE,
As an elegant lyrics to music rustled in the breeze
As genuine riveting melody of LOVE affair
As my LOVE ebb and sweeps back to flow
As the wave of endless ocean,
As I am never without you, My Darling
My Beloved eternal ebullient poetic muse

MY LOVE RESTS ON HEART OF MY
BELOVED,
IT IS AN ENDLESS OCEAN OF DEVOTION ,
WITH NO BEGINNING OR END

Come to my seashore of LOVE
My Darling,
As I am drenched

in the Flood of Your LOVE
Please come to me , My LOVE,
I will promise to open
the flooded gate of my HEART

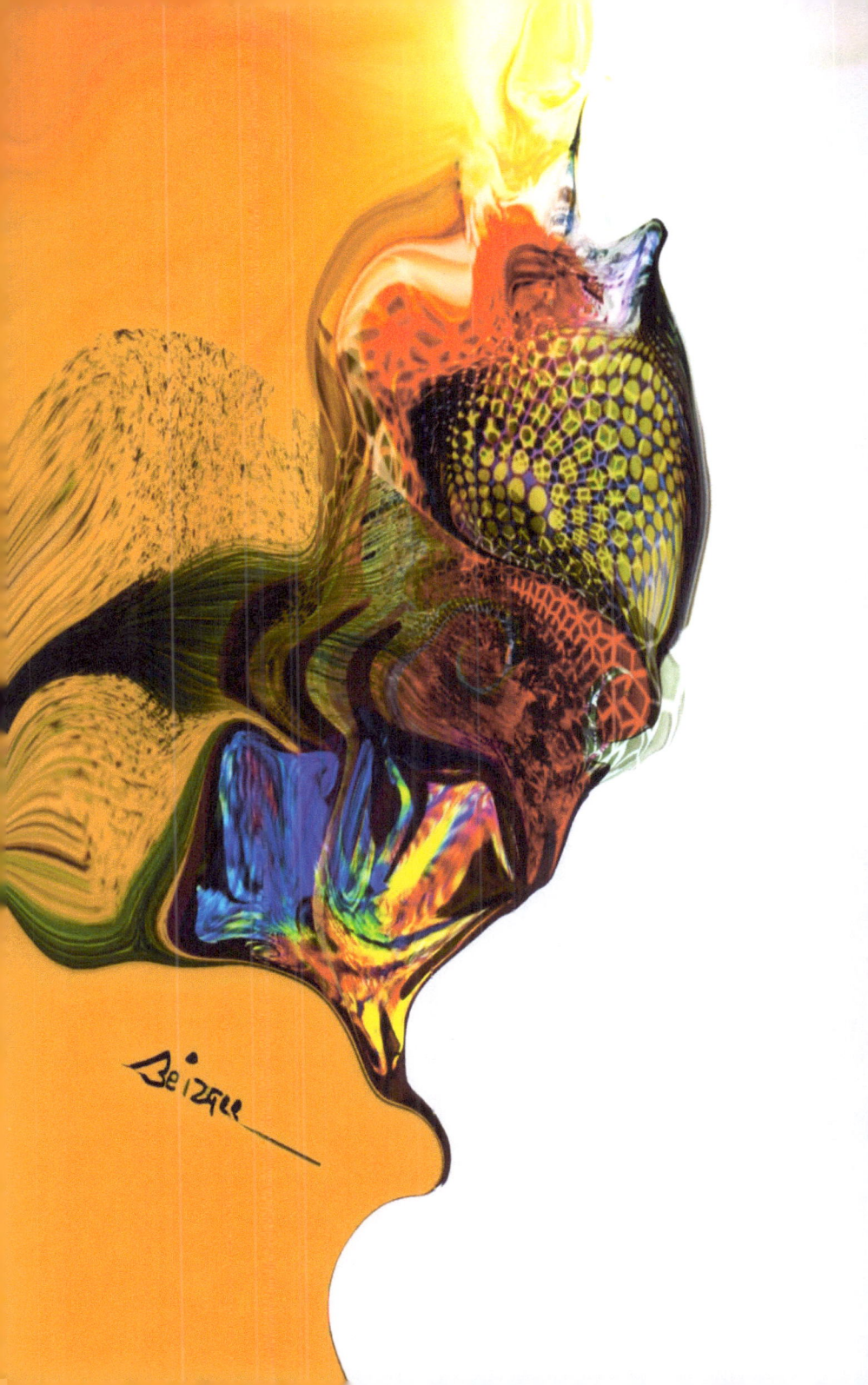

Love Poems

My Longing Tears

My longing tears are the temple
Of thousands LOVERS whom
Worshiping the name of LOVE
Utterly Blissed with Exaltation
And Ecstasy without fear or Shame

In the twilight of My beloved
Longing , my innocent pearl
My other self ,
My immortal tears
Spill from my propitious eyes
As procession of hope
Gone by the parade of Tears
replacing the phantom of harmonies,

ah, Its so painful
ah, well-away
CARESSES MY ALONENESS FACE
AS BARTERED VEIL OF LOVE
For Heartless salt
As the song of FORGOTTEN Rivulets

THE SOUL OF TEARS Whispers
LOVE ONCE WHOLLY
LOVE ONCE SUBLIME
LOVE ONCE BLISSFUL

AS LOVE Gazes upon Itself
In the Mirror Of TEARS
As my LIPS Bathe in TEARS
Hidden in the Splendors of
BITTER FLOODS

ah, its so bitter
ah, well-away
As LIPS Drinks from
The river Of SILENCE

HOW WILL THIS EXQUISITE
BENEVOLENT HUMBLE
TEARS OF LOVE
Hence Sweep back to ease
My INTOXICATED
MAJESTIC TENDER LOVE
MY EVERY REASON OF BEING?

IF THOU HAST NOT SEEN
MY TEARS On my Face
As Mirror of ALL MOMENTS,
Darkling valleys
Of buried LOVE on my LIPS
Drinking our IMMORTAL
Moment Of SOLITUDE

Where the tales of Tranquility
Once translucent as
TRUMPETING TWO MERGED
SOULS UNDER TWO LIPS
UTTERLY AS ONE
Kindled the Valley Of
Begotten LOVE STORY?

WOULD YOUR FORGOTTEN LIPS
Whispers my name JUST ONCE?
Lay my Thoughts JUST ONCE?
Bury my HEART JUST ONCE?
As in a SEPULCHER as once
Stood in the ground Of LOVE
SO HOLY As BELOVED SANCTUARY
To DECORATE MY WORLD
AS URN ASHES Of MY LOVE

Love Poems

Mother

Mother,
The sacred minister of LOVE,
My Temple of tenderness,
Your boundless tender hearted
bountiful river of endearment , nurtures
to cultivate the flower of my soul,
Mother,
My savior, My soul is born on the shore
Of your benevolent loving eyes
Quivering with your loving chants
Mother,
My loving paradise of serenity,
Your heart has opened the gate
Of the garden of LOVE
Upon my arrival, as I came
As shadow to reside in your Loving heart
Mother,
My sanctuary of gentleness,
My companion of my darkest hours,
Your Loving eyes illuminate
the Devine promise of bliss

As every act of your kindness
As the ebb and flow
in the ocean of my heart
As your Love notes floats
to the surface of my heart in rivulets

Mother,
The infinite tender majesty,
The touch of your blossoming heart
Convey as profound elixir to heal
my deepest wounds, quenching
the anguished flame of life,
Mother,
I LOVE YOU,
my heart would not feel complete
without You,
I LOVE Your tender lips
As silky sheen blanket of tenderness
And I will never forget
When My face was
a basket of your warm kisses

Mother; My tent of Love,
Your Beloved hands are best LOVED
They have reached out for my hands
every time I am about to fall,
Your Beloved hands,
has blessed my reason of being
and guarded my heart
as the fortitude of LOVE
Your Beloved hands,
thought me how to build
a swing of LOVE in the backyard
of our hearts to write LOVE songs

and to decorate the walls
with pride and beauty
in majestic colors of red and blue crayon
Mother,
My faithfullest Beloved companion,
I missed our time together,
I LOVE YOU but I missed you,
If I have not said it enough,
Please forgive me Mother,
Thank you for Loving me,
Utterly, I am all yours,
and I LOVE YOU dearly and dearly forever,
As I lift my heart to you,
the grace and wisdom is poured,
they have clung to me all my life,

Mother, you are LOVE,
and LOVE is a tender hands
of every Mother that sways
in every direction and finds
heart to give in its blissfulness
As sways to weave the fabric of life,
Mother,
I LOVE YOU,
Thank YOU for every breath you gave me
when I was your BELOVED
in YOUR LOVING Womb
Mother,
My Beloved Temple of Tenderness,
Your Loving compassion poured light
Into the cup of my heart to teach me
the illumination of majestic LOVE
as I got nourished by your utmost
benevolent unconditional gracious LOVE.

LOVE Vows

As we stand hand in hand
As the wings of LOVE
enfold our hearts as ONE
under the arboresque
Majesty Of LOVE
Utterly at the ineffable abode
Under the trellis bower of our hearts
As the innocent image of LOVE
emanate clearly as ONE
behind the effulgence veil of life

As we stand,
in the glory of LOVE
face to face,
As our eyes wed
in the illustrious honorable
Majestic name of LOVE
As our souls, as ONE
Meditating LOVE
in the Temple of LOVE
to inhabit songs
ruminating LOVE's elation

As we stand in awe
of the Kingdom of LOVE
As to drink LOVE
from the limpid river of heart
As joined together, as the sea of LOVE
where our hearts is waiting groom
and our memories an eternal wedding to bloom
Let us choose LOVE
to be awakening between us
Let there be a sacred space
between the Temples of our souls
that the Angels of Heaven roam to witness
the serenity, LOVE and tenderness

Let there be a space of solitude
As a veil between us to scape the
confinement and constraint of our egos
Let there be a space for exultation
of our spirits in the shadow of passion
Let there be a space where our hearts
may speak without words

Let there be a space in our hearts
to build the tallest tower of LOVE,
The Temple of Forgiveness,
Let us build the tower of Forgiveness
with our devotion and tenderness

Let us climb up, hand in hand
To reach the summit of LOVE,
at the peak to prospect our sunrise
of our LOVE once again, hand in hand
Let there be a space in our hearts
As the Temple of Ecstasy

to prance on the red horse of LOVE
to the path of our hearts , where LOVE
is bowing to our purity
and simplicity of our LOVE

Let us memorize the name of LOVE
to draw a picture of LOVE
in our souls with red fountain pen of LOVE
Let us place a mirror in our hearts
to reflect the purity of our tenderness
Let us pray LOVE
Let us wake up with LOVE
Let us make LOVE
To intense fragility of LOVE
forcing our ways to the peak of bliss
intensifying our veiled desires

We pledge,
in the purity and tenderness of LOVE
We pledge,
to the majesty of LOVE
to intense fragility of LOVE
to the gentleness of our spirits
to LOVE each other for eternity
Utterly, completely
to intense fragility of LOVE
to honor our hearts
to honor our souls
to intense fragility of LOVE
to promise our togetherness
to believe in us
to intense fragility of LOVE
to believe in our
blissful, tender, sublime

Devine swoon of our LOVE
To intense fragility of LOVE

Let us stretch our hands
as a symbol of giving
We stretch our right hands
To touch our hearts
As the Temple of LOVE

As filled with limpid
eternal fountain of LOVE
to feel and hear each beat
of its purity and devotion

We hold our left hands together
as unity, as oneness
as wholeness and completeness
of our hearts in evocation of our endless
sublime LOVE
Let us rejoice and give songs and Hymns
of praise as the spirit of OUR LOVE ascends
In delight scenes of jubilation among Beloveds

Our Vow,
As our Oneness heart, Utters
As a LOVE citty song of hymn
As the foam of LOVE, paints
Its adorable face of LOVE story
on the shores of our hearts

Our Vow,
Shall make our heart Throne
And LOVE a sovereign crown
of our destiny

The Season Of LOVE

Now that the season of LOVE
has come set me free
in the time of LOVE
from repentance
As tears of forgiveness
Shall washout the word Of penitence
to an evocation of spiritual solace
Now that the season of LOVE
has come let us pray to sweeten
the bread of bitterness among us
Now that the season of LOVE
has come let us share
the feast of LOVE
on the rug of our loneliness
Let us sing loud
the song of our silence
Let us immerse LOVE
In the heart of loneliness
Let us exchange an ear of forgiveness
that could only hear the courageous
Devine Thunder of blissfulness
Empathy, LOVE and ONENESS

Love Touched Me

LOVE touched me
And the unlit wick
Of my HEART became
A sacred flame of bliss
In the endless
Sea of emptiness
Pulsated light throughout
the center point
Of Heaven
As effulgent might
As LOVE Enwrought
With coronet
As I SAW GOD
IN MY HEART

The Blanket Of LOVE

(In the Memory Of Holocaust Victims)

Once upon the time
In the Kingdom of Forest
The Ancient holy trees
Growing in humanity
Fragrance of unity
Climbed up, as poems that
leaves writes upon the sky;
"Their Fruits shall be for food
And their leaves for healing"

The colorful leaves lithely
remain the cheerful
trumpet of miraculous life
Heralding with its melodic tune
Played gracefully, shared
Laughter adroitly, loved blissfully
A vicious thunder of hate

Collapse upon the Kingdom of forest
From the West,
Come forth violence of hate
From the North,
Like pool of fear quivering
From the South,
The fluttering of lids darkness the eyes
From the East,
Storm of tormented souls

The trunk of the trees
Becomes colorless
Indifferent and ignorance
As silent storm in solitude
To let go, the flexible
Caring loving branches
As MOTHER, as TENDERNESS
Holds its Beloved child,
As Leaves, gaze in Thine own Heart

AS MANY AS SIX MILLION
MAKES A NOISE FALLING
A NOSTALGIC HEROISM
LAYING IN THE GRAVE
COVERED IN PETALS OF
IGNOMINY AND INJUSTICE
PERCHANCE TO DREAM
AS THEIR VOICE OF LIFE
COULD NOT REACH
THE EAR OF LIFE

As deception being praised
It becomes a song
That rises from a bleeding
As Churlish defiance

As the sky sank to grief
Fell like unstoppable
Tears of shame
Wiping out the sun
Into black solitude of darkness

As agony of trench warfare
With voice of despair
Wondering and grieving
Kingdom of Forest
WITHOUT LEAVES
Is always lonely
With its sad pure silence
TEARS IS ITS FIFE

THE YELLOW STAR LEAVES
WOVEN THE BLANKET OF LOVE
FROM THE ASHES
WHOSE DREAMS AND LIVES
WERE STOLEN AWAY

Strewed the Graveyard of
Hopeless shame
To decorate and waver
Their Melody Of Love
As the candlelight of
FALLEN HUMANITY

Wavered in the draft
As murmuring
As their lips and wind

Wed in eternal Sublime
KISSING
FAREWELL
OUR
BELOVED
BENEVOLENT
HEROES

The Trees feel
Naked as Shame

As their hearts become
Stream river of Ignorance
Running as Churlish defiance

The Ancient Tree of Life
Bewildered as dethroned King
By its diminutive etymology
Renounced the Kingdom of dreams
Fell down and TURN into PAPER
THAT WE MAY RECORD EMPTINESS
AS WISDOM FOR ETERNITY,
NEVER AGAIN
NEVER AGAIN
As The Yellow Star Leaves
Woven the blanket of LOVE
From the ashes
Whose dreams and Lives
We're stolen away.

Forgiveness

Let's roam in the garden of heart
to plant the tallest tree of Forgiveness
Let's revive our faithfulness to LOVE
as forgiveness revives our heart to LOVE
as ignorance as innocence of past
Best shrouded in shadows we casts
as Lovers plighted their troth
as fecund deity to repose our souls
to refresh our hearts under the shadows
of boundless love, in a silent rendezvous
as cognizance as innocence of past
Best shrouded in shadows we casts
Let's cherish our heart with every fiber
of our soul to cherish the majesty of LOVE
Let's immerse our souls in the river
of absolution to wash the sweat of forgiveness
as our Devine retribution
Let's build a castle of the forgiveness
With the silky sheen hands of tenderness
With the velvety , sumptuous sweat of our souls
Let's build a castle of forgiveness
To wed the reign of forgiveness
To the crown of our hearts.

Your Loving touch

Your benevolent touch
Borrowed courage to reach
my Heart to break the shells of
my loneliness to bleed LOVE
Willingly and joyfully to liberate
my heart to be winged
to fly to the holy temple of LOVE
to heal the wounds of my own
understanding of LOVE as you touched
me without even Being touched
YOUR Healing Glimmered Every Atom
Of MY BEING SO Deeply Liberating
my joyful rivulets of tears down
my flesh comforting my SOUL

The Attainment

Each single SOUL
An epitome of
Goodness and LOVE
complexity but elegance
Imprisoned for Attainment
Is a true Prince as steadfast
Immortal flame of LOVE
Anointed by GOD
Shall find his Throne
In the Heart Of Egoless
Timeless, Blissful LOVE

LOVE enfolds forgiveness

Love enfolds it's bravery story
As a merciful ruler
As a great spirit to tote
the water of life's heart
from the sea of Love
As a great spirit to tote
the water of life's agony
from the river of silence,
Leave the garment
of mercilessness
in the river of imperiousness
and wash your nakedness
with holy water of Love
to forgive the bitterness
of ego and pridefulness

Have you lost LOVE
in the hidden flood of
your pride and ego
flowing with the darkness of

Love's sunset?
Then pursue the map of
Love, step by step
Marching in lockstep
with affection and hymn
Then behold,
As your Beloved eyes
Seized the tender heart
As the fragility of LOVE
become the royal noble preserve
with gentle handwill beckon
from Heart to LOVE
to see the gentle Lovers
determined to uncling
the past innocent wounds
As LOVE's footstep shadows
Silently kneeling in the grace of mercifulness
Compassionate rhythm of Divine hearts,

And witness to seek Lovers best portray fabrics
of fragility with locks of LOVE ascending in folds
with devotion and tenderness
to the tallest tower of LOVE;
"The Forgiveness",
As the Prince and Princes
are LOVE
As their heirs are;
salvation, vindication and sanctification
As their breeds are;
Pardon, amnesty and remission

Vanished into LOVE

The amber Fiery blistering
Candle of EGO whispering
Luring words with Seductive lips
Dancing by Haughty disdain
Eglantine and Amber
As blue strenuous earthy
Jasmin scented Candle of
HEART cries for Jubilation
In climax flowing sublime
Pearls of HUMANITY
To sing the song of Our silence
As twirling away from EGO
Intoxicated with SALVATION
To dance LOVE Devoutly
In EUPHORIA MELTING EGO
To BLISS Farewell
As glowing With Tranquility
And Passion As VANISHED INTO LOVE
In pure ECSTASY SUBLIME
Everlasting Elation Of LOVE

Open thine own Heart

Immerse in the tranquility of truth
And believe in the opulence of your
Devine being , BEHOLD IT,
As the proof You seek is THOU
As Heaven's Breath of Spiritual eloquence
As an Infinite horizon
In the radiance of light of Heaven
As beyond Yourself
As LOVE with Conscious intent
In the waves of Tenderness
Ascending and Receding
To return to the Egoless light

Behold,
Open the gate of your Heart
To witness the fountain of LOVE
The redeeming endless flow
That reconciles LOVE to life

Dear wandering pilgrim,
The gate keeper Of HEART,
BLEED THE WATER OF LOVE
EAGERLY and BLISSFULLY
TO CLEANSE
THE WORLD IMPURITIES
And give gratitude to let the Fountain
Of Purity, Kindness and Tenderness
      Trail the robe of Bliss and Glory
TO BESTOW LOVE,
HUMANITY And COMPASSION
Until YOU REMEMBER
that YOU are "LOVE"
THE ULTIMATE HEALER
THE ULTIMATE
MANIFESTATION OF TRUE LOVE
THE TRUE SUBLIME CREATION OF LOVE

The Sunrise of LOVE

Omnipresent Devine sublime body
of light, which its passionate lips
folds many sacred other worlds
As I am compelled to ink
a secret on this page
As a twinkle promise
As oceans of LOVE are drawn
From our well of tenderness heart
Our heart trampling out
the purifying fire of Divinity
As LOVE faith the everlasting troth
under the sublime sacred thundering
beauty of The Tree Of Life
where the fruits of salvation are
harvested in The Temple of LOVE
Under the eyes of LOVE
waiting to be anointed
As LOVE anoints its hand
to touch the face of one who ached
Beware as you gaze into every heart

on this earth, you see LOVE
is the Beloved of all hearts
GOD, The Supreme Beloved,
The Holy One, Blessed Be HE,
Constructed an extraordinary
Temple Of LOVE in every atom of heart
As our heart is the true
inheritance of Devine LOVE
As all atoms in existence
are universally in LOVE
And at each Devine juncture
the heart of atom expands
its wing to touch LOVE
intimately under the judgment of LOVE
waiting to be anointed like heavenly bodies
As our LOVE promises
the bright spark of Divinity
LOVE's pure face has revealed
its beauty to us, utterly, this is a delighted
Treasure and NOT hidden, Behold
As LOVE binds
As prudence, patient and perseverance
And bounds as temperance
As celestial spheres of Heaven
And LOVE is NOT hidden
It is simply in our heart
As dim and flaring
majestic lamps of heart
As LOVE is an imperial
Friend of heart
Sovereign of itself
As LOVE is the ultimate

Tender Majesty and dwells
In the harmony of eternal Divinity
As begotten to devote oneself
to the deity to become ONE
with everything as total ONENESS
as the emblem of eternity
As LOVE unfurled its majesty
As the innermost hidden
treasure of creation
As the golden seed of the
Temple Of LOVE
As a Devine bride in our heart
As LOVE is the deed of universe
As LOVE is the birth certificate
Of immortals as dance of Devine
sacred realm of enchantment
As LOVE is a sacred container
As blissed Devine elixir
which contains the wisdom of Heaven
driven by the self-emancipation
Opulence eye of devotion
And GOD's LOVE
Is the wedding gift
for our Devine union
And giving LOVE
is the ring of wedding

Heart

Dost Thy soul's inner majesty
Ponder Thy heart's purity
Hath the eyes of LOVE blossoms
the effulgence of Thy heart's flowers
Thou art the heart's gatekeeper
As the milk of Divine kindness
To gild refined royalty of kingliness
To the majestic towering passion
of LOVE, as Thy heart's mirror
Shalt never forget Thy Beloved face
As the moon's visage
Captivated the yearning flote
As the tender majestic jubilation of light
encompasses the endless ocean of heart
As illuminating as prescient of grace
Lured with allure
As blissful begotten pearl of LOVE
As the tender arms of LOVE
As enchanting fortitude of delight fete
Illuminating the Divine gage of glee

As riveting as bird of gallant venturous desire
As passionate invocation of rapturous sublime
As Beloved muse of LOVE
Heralding with its utmost poetic tune
As begotten sacred balm of life
As pure prophetic ebullient of LOVE

The Infinite

Hath Thy heart behooves
As spotless mirror to reveal
Its innocence as limpid river of sooth
to emanate Divine light of LOVE
Hath Thy LOVE
Kindled Thy Loving heart
As an ebullient glimmering
effulgence smileth of traveling
lamp to cross the bridge of abyss
As Thy vibrant heart
intoxicated with the Infinite
As it shalt be the Divine
Fluttering pulse seekers
As the phantom of delight
As the arboretum of immortality
sweeping the path of selflessness
into greatened bilboes of eternity
As we art anchored to the Infinite
Evoking the enchantment of the
LOVE Story in the purity of heart

in tribulation joy, as Thy heart
bestowed LOVE, TEN Lights
spring forth from LOVE midst
As Divine light emanating sooth
As festive celebrating joy
As map of consciousness
As Thy heart is shedding its
Leaves as utterance of deeds
As raiment Vatic grandeur flames
of sovereign majestic greatness

In The Kingdom Of Hearts
Whence the golden seeds
of Divinity did create the
riveting sublime name of LOVE
Whence the Majestic name of LOVE
Hath been did praise for eternity

Whence the veil of Hearts revealed
its eyeless secrets to shine and glorify
the effulgence and resplendence
image of ONENESS
Whence the visage of LOVE
Hath been an exalted refulgence
Aura of sanctitude and reverence
Whence the heart of universe
is begotten as rapturous vibrant of unity
As an ebullient purity of LOVE
Whence every heart of atom
As utmost sublime image of LOVE
Is bowing to intense fragility of LOVE
to praise The Supreme Beloved

GOD, The Holy One Bless Be HE
The Only Beloved Signifier
Whom hath unified LOVE
in harmony as grain of every being
As the most precious adoring dazzling
Benevolent effulgent riveting
Light as sublime, abiding and enduring
As The Heart bestowed LOVE
TEN Lights spring forth from LOVE
Metaphor scenes under the
Wings Of LOVE art to be born
As allegory into word of Heart
As the Holy Ancient one
As the wilt of wills soar up
The booketh of Supreme wilt
by two wings of Awe and LOVE
As Heavens saluted the
CROWNing majesty of Divine LOVE

As all engraving of LOVE started
As sacred word abridged
Within single point of WISDOM
As the breath of Life is the palace
of soul buildeth by the limpid
rivulets of awareness as womb
of LOVE as tacit UNDERSTANDING
of the Divine traits of cosmos

As the seeds of LOVE as GREATNESS
poems of majesty and bloom
As last vestiges of Royal POWER
As the nobility of tenderness swords

of justice, integrity and virtue
As its BEAUTY harmonizes
ENDURANCE as the castle of hearts
Rises in solidarity SPLENDOR
on the fringed enlightenment
spirit of heart as the foundation
Of LOVE is of The Supreme Beloved
GOD, The HOLY ONE ,Bless
Be HE, The Only Beloved Signifire

As the whisper of Divinity
As riveting as melodious
Elegance blissful birth of heart
As rapturous vibrant
ebullient portrait of LOVE
As eternal poetic sound
Smites upon the ear of LOVE
As LOVE rules the KINGDOM
Of all hearts without a Sword.

Inception Of LOVE

From the inception of riveting
Majestic Tale Of LOVE
To tinge of intense devotion
Confide the secrets of creation
As illuminating as enticing mystic souls
As fluttering splendorous opulence
Light Of LOVE piercing the
Chamber of ineffable limpid Heart
with silent steps in secret meekness
As elixir of life flowing from the
blossomed truest wisdom of healing Heart
As pledged kiss of promise to induce LOVE
As an exultant elated bond of enduring
coherent continuum of unity
As the cosmic symbolism of LOVE
Encircling in eternity
in transfixing touch of LOVE
As gentle chivalrous Swordsmen Of Truth
As Chariest Commencement Inception Of LOVE
As delight phantom of enchantment

As affection galore suffuse
As souls ebullient poetic muse
As catalyst of sublime fulfillment
As genuine amiable boisterous reunion
As rambunctious dance of Immortal

As reciting lyrical Hymn-book of LOVE
As promising of prophetic utterance
guffawed with delight to one epoch
To surge veritable plaque of Brotherhood
To reconcile and unite by ;
Crowning The Grace Of Humanity
Doth NOT Liveth in bondage Lured by
lust, envy, covetousness, pride and spleen.

LOVE's Sword of tenderness shalt purify
the fire of Ego as being embowelled
reverentially as befits defunct embers
of lust's funeral pyre
As compassion of Heart shalt nurtures
Caprice as all sentient of being
The justice of LOVE shalt purges
Defilement to buckler off
the Mother Of Impudence
To sweeten the torment of feigned
Ignorance as LOVE anoints
the sanctify vessel of Heart.

Thou shalt heareth ONLY the LOVE's
Utterance, the Voice within
To redeem truth, harmony and ONENESS
As our innocent sublime Souls

Appease to pause to its silhouette
As our Hearts bloom to shelter
the splendid shadow of LOVE
To restore harmony of ONENESS
To pledge to placate to unite Hearts
And plume up the Majestic
Benevolent name of LOVE

Thou shalt heareth the words of Truth
As Thou art solemnly the tender
Majesty Of LOVE ,
The true inheritance Visage Of Divine
Light ; the pure fabric of blithe light
Woven in the Citadel Of Elysium.
The Supremacy of Heart uttering
The Inception Of LOVE
By the voice of contentment
To ignite Souls flames of Devotion
To endure the labyrinth of Tribulation,
Agony and affliction
As the Heart's wisdom endure
The burning purifying fire Of LOVE
To cast the shadow of Ego
To illuminate Heart as radiance moon
As the Majestic Kingdom Of Heart
Hath Vexation from the Universe
In utmost Supreme unity
As Thy enthralling adoring Heart
Delve too deeply into Soul's
Truest pearl of Wisdom ,
To Kiss the promise of UNITY.

The Inception Of LOVE
As The Majestic Towering Of Passion
Whispering the Hymn Of Souls
in encircling Eternity
To gaze upon the innermost
HEART of all Beloveds.

Secret Place

Hath the sunset of LOVE
Fluttered Thy Beloved Heart
in grief and bewilderment
As the effulgence Wings Of LOVE
glints of the Sea Of LOVE
Whence LOVE weeps its
Rivulets Of Pearls as its
Milky sheen tassels rose
Petals of beauty liveth in thorn
And its petals hast thousands lips
But nay one can heareth
its thousands secrets
Cometh with me to a secret
seashore of Thy LOVE
Whence Thy Beloved Heart
is the infinite flote and its every
Heart beat is a LOVE Note
in every drop of its water

Cometh with me to a secret
Place in Thy Heart, as Thou shalt
close Thy Beloved Heart's Lips
in peace and wait enduringly for LOVE
to cometh to ope its crimson Lips
by the eternal kiss of liberation
Cometh with me to a secret
Place in Thy Heart whence
Thy Beloved Heart shalt
Becometh the Chief Justice Of LOVE
Whence the bodkins Of Truth
and tenderness becometh ONE Bodkin
As the indomitable Pious Chronicle
Of all Hearts waiting impatiently
to embrace The LOVE Of HUMANITY
Whence LOVE's Sword Of Tenderness
Cuts the umbilical cord of Thy birth
To blaze all thorns of Life to unburden
And purify Thy Beloved Heart's
Mirror of passion to reflect and
To reveal Thy true Thou

Cometh with me to a secret lodging
in our minds, as only LOVERS
shalt findeth Whence Thy Judgment is
THE POINT OF HEART
Whence the query about LOVE
is victoriously sealed in the Heart
of Grace and delicacy Of LOVE
Whence the connection to LOVE
Is not fragile nor secret any more AND
Thither is nay needeth of mine Poetry AND

Haply I shouldst grise out and step out
Of Thy Beloved Mind's Heart
Since THOU ART THE SECRET
PLACE and indeed,
THOU ART THE HEART of
LOVE which hath dupp all its gates
To bleed most wondrous streams of
Limpid Crystals Of Water Of LOVE
To trail the Robe Of Bliss And Glory.

The Anatomy Of Heart

Heart,
The Temple Of Light
Clothed in the kiss of LOVE
As glittering sublime waves
Birthing twilight's Majesty
As a luminous effulgence vessel
To witness pulsating poems
To parse the plenum
As the gage of Divinity
As the acme of perfection
As the Light's cordial greeting
Parity with heart as rapturous
applause manifestation of the Infinite
as solemn invocation breath
Of Loving devoting kind prayer
Uplifted by LOVE as recompense
Gift of yearning as mesmerizing
As cloaking the soul in most liberating
embrace of Divinity as the whole universe
Is ensteeped in oceans of Heart's

mystifying enigmatic eyes as the triumphal
pearl of wisdom dripped into her eyes
As the journey of Light hath begotten
As harmonious hymn of LOVE
To only one point of wisdom, The
oneness of Divine Supreme Beloved.
The Majesty of Heart,
The treasure chest of soul,
The secret dwelling lodging of LOVE
The journey of ineffable radiant light
Upon light delve into the secret of LOVE
In the vessel of oneness, as the Divine kiss
Sanctifies light as the poetic graze
Endearment, as inspires stars to ascend
into sky and gambol to light up the
Universe in the delights of Elysium
As lights upon lights dances to gage
The Majestic signature of Devine
As what the soul hath seen in heavenly
Realm of Heart, as an abide of perfect
Blessedness, as a true revelation of ONENES

As Heart is an endless curtain of abodes
As four faced glass of limpid sky on horizons
and the eyes of Heart as an impish
Sophistication only matched by its innocent
As a Devine mirror of reflection manifest
in the Higher celestial realm in eternal rotation
Thither art two kingdoms , Ego and LOVE
Face to Face in the innermost Majesty
Of Heart casting their gaze as wading
In the Sea of LOVE.

In the Garden of Heart
Heart's minister of the interior ,
An enclosure of infinite in extent
holds the Garden Of Union
Whence the trees art blossomed
With justice, prudence, fortitude, faith,
Temperance, hope, charity, pity, patience
And Shalt remain in the infinite streams
of Truth, Whence the seekers of LOVE
Shalt immerse in the unity streams
As harbors many rivers of absolution
As the light of LOVE pouring into the
Infinite Oceans Of LOVE , embraced
By The Temple Of Forgiveness ,
Soul's chief nemesis,
the tallest towers of lights.
In The Kingdom Of Ego, the province of
Conspicuous towers of annealed
Haughtiness rests The Castle Of Desires,
the unrequited LOVE of vanity
as depth beyond depth of darkness
hath revealed the Six Hundred Twenty
Houses Of Abyss, as Intractable
establishment of Lust, Pride, avarice,
Gluttony, ire, mendacious, envy, …
As blandishment light of darkness.
In The Kingdom Of LOVE,
The Temple Of Awakening,
The Chamber Of Accession
to The Throne Of Supreme Beloved
As the pilgrimage light of Union
Shalt bewray the Truth

As the veil of sooth is torn
from the priceless ultimate treasure
As the blissed path to rejoice the Beloved
As an effulgence riveting lights embracing
As fluttering Of mating birds uttering
its ebullient hearty,
As the tinkling hymn of unity
holds Seven Castles;
The Castles Of Devotion , Radiance , purity
Merit , LOVE , Goodwill , UNITY and holds
Five worlds of soul's consciousness
to smelleth the fragrance of wisdom.
As the act of universe enters
The Majesty Of Heart , as the light ,
Thy Beloved soul as the light of Divinity
Cleaves to the act, as bestowal
For the benefits of other souls with
Recompense to be rewarded
Or haply thou shalt desire to sweep
the ancient dust of desires by
an abyss of infinite depth,
then certes thy soul shalt be
in The Kingdom Of Ego,
As thy soul relinquishes pleasure
As bestow in charge to bestow
As to giveth LOVE and tender kindness
Merely tending to the betterment of others,
then certes thy soul shalt be
in The Kingdom Of LOVE.

As the light of Ego bonds to thy soul,
In The Kingdom Of Ego,

Beware of many visage of altruistic desires
As the master taint of light shalt shed
its darkest recess as did consort
tergiversation lustful, haughtiest's gaffe
A sinister spin stain on thy soul whence the
Light is imperishable to findeth midline of life,
As the light of LOVE expands thy soul,
In The Kingdom Of LOVE,
As the Oceans Of LOVE, the ambits of
Limitless boundaries encompasses
the world of delight benevolent light
to the breadth of infinity,
As the Truth is incontrovertible daughter
of time the ultimate redeemer of perfection
consciousness, as reconciles LOVE
to conquer it's celestial promise of bliss.
Thou shalt breaketh the shackles
of desires which shed its ignorance
As the journey from the separation of
The Kingdom Of Ego into the union of self
To free Thy soul as the seekers of unity
And submerge in the bridge of light
Crossing the house of abyss to
Enter The Kingdom Of LOVE
Whence the rapture of the truth unfolds
As The Supreme Beloved Divine Light
Crisps a ring 'round Thy soul
As opening its petals to the hymn of Divinity.

Thou shalt at each moment
whisper to recall ;
Thou art marry the sublime Cosmic

Divine light In The bower Of eternity
An eternal flame of fervent LOVE
As Five Pearls Of Thy Souls did
Join By string of Divinity ,
Bestow LOVE to rendezvous The radiant
ineffable light Of Supreme Beloved
At The Gate Of UNITY,
The Sacrosanct shrine of perfect blessedness
Whence the triumphant of soul shalt kiss
to cleave the Divine Sword Of
The Supreme Beloved by an eternal
Knot of sooth, as blessing in motion
As the sacred pilgrimage center of light,
Whence the One Hundred Twenty Five
Steps of Spiritual Ascent toward attainment
Starts as the infinite kiss of LOVE unites souls
As accepting the yolk of Heavens
As true revelation of ONENESS.

Loving Souls

LOVE hath passionate fevers
to revive the royalty of Hearts
As the conveyance vessels
of endearment crosses its lips
As the tender swords of righteous
Kiss, as the effulgence impulses
of sacrifice, as the fragile tenderness
fiber of Heart hath sowed the seeds
of LOVE, as fastened by kinship ties
utterly affixed near propinquity of souls
As the champion voice of Lovers
Hath The Divine Pearls Of Ballads
To dance its blood grumes
To the flame of yearning LOVE Hymns
As cascading unwavering vigor eagerness
As lurks in all delights

Emilia , Ethan ;
My Dualistic Immortal Beloveds
Fortress Of Life ;
As the Book Of LOVE

Engraves the tale of LOVE
THY LOVE Shalt Shine
From the ebullient Phantom Of LOVE
As an egoless majestic vibrant colorful Rainbow
As an awe-inspiring Castle in the air
As smiles Thy Beloved names at both ends
As its spirit shalt span Thy heavenly spheres names
As two bloomed floret baskets of LOVE Kisses
As gallant , as blissful cognizant fearless
Heedful LOVE epithets, as Burgeoning Empire
to radiate the fragrance of sweetness
effloresce flower of compassion
As The Queen and The King of Hearts
Promulgate a decree as, the serenity
And merriment hold its seeds with much hilarity
And mirth, as it shalt inspires the Stars
To ascend and climb The Garden Of LOVE
Into the secret lips of the sky to kiss back
And light up Thy precious faces, as exhibiting the
Spectacular emulations of extravagance with Kisses

Emilia and Ethan,

Thou art the endless grace of elegance
Thy mellifluous names as an emollient
Pearl petals of LOVE flower gently settles
Evoking felicitous whim to wear smileth
On Thy Beloved faces
As the delicate blankets of tenderness
Opens its petals wide as the murmurous
Red rose Of LOVE wink at the celestial
dimensions of Thy beauties
My creed is deeply sown with tenderness

notion, as an allegiant affectionate Father,
inspired by LOVE, guided by wisdom and
devoured by the flame of Devotion.
Thou art the endless grace of elegance
Thy Beloveds Benevolent touch
As riveting sublime petals of tender rose
As kindle Majesty of kindness
As the fervid resplendence rising nobleness Of Life,
As murmuring glorious fruits of our wisdom
As the seeds of LOVE pulverized into
Beauteous perfect amity of tenderness
As soft, pellucid delicate epiphany
Growing on Crimson Crown of Hearts
With kisses soft as butterflies trembling
and swaying to the Hymn Of LOVE
On Thy taut stems, as the caress of Thy
Beloveds touch begets my heart open forever

Emilia and Ethan,

Thou shalt lift Thy Beloveds Hearts solemnly
to eminent exalted Majestic Divinity Of LOVE
As vivid evocative colorful sobriquet
As Triumphal marching hymns of Hearts
As rumination elation of meditating Hearts
Uttered as praise in effusive floods of Hymns
As Pure limpid sublime melody of beating Hearts
As singing the muse Divine afflatus
Of The Beloveds souls to resonate
With the ambrosial melodies of the Elysium
As an opulent Divine siren interweaving
the arras of enigmatic LOVE STORY
As we art oblige to embrace

The majestic Supremacy Of LOVE with
our ope hands and ope hearts
Our Hearts hath spoken truly under the
Arboresque tranquility of LOVE as enduring
Fluttering begotten wings of innocent LOVE
To emanate in sublimity as ONENESS
Divinity Of GOD hath revealed its Eternal Glory
Behind the effulgence Veil Of LOVE

Emilia and Ethan;

Thou shalt witness the bond of ONENESS
the ultimate golden seed ,
the sacred secret of LOVE ,
As its immense Majestic bliss hath enliven
and enlighten our imaginations and dreams
As the chambers of Thy Beloveds Hearts
Keeps opening to witness the wilt of Truth
As the Melody Of LOVE shalt be the
Sword Of Tenderness at which hour
the Veil Of Heart Of Hearts
shalt bewray the Concealment,
As the Majestic Name Of LOVE
Shalt bow to intense fragility of Heart
To praise the ONENESS Of GOD
As The First and Last Hymn Of ONENESS
As rapturous ecstasy of exalted Jubilation
As the anointed eyes of LOVE
Hath attested the concealed Pearl Of Wisdom
In the Sea Of Limpid Eternal DIVINE LOVE

Emilia and Ethan;

Hark to Thy Loving Souls as speaks
As the true delight enchanting radiance light
As sovereign master of Heart's earthly blissed
Province, shalt dance as the dread desire leaps
into flame Of LOVE and let Thy Beauteous Eternal
Souls Slink Like earthly grains of sands between
The Fingers of LOVE as it slips from Light Of
Divinity to the Candle Of Heart, as each soul finds
Slipping again and again to oblige and applaud
to inspire Heart in its meridian height as it clings
to the effulgence radiant sublime light of
The Supreme Beloved Of LOVE
Thy Beloveds Hearts keeps opening to the
Trumpet of joy as the fortitude Of LOVE
As pure innocent limpid pungent Civet Of Eternity
Thy Beloveds LOVE as sweet faith of blossomed
Beehives Of Honey to attest LOVE Of Heart
As Honey, much more sweeter than Thousand
Glorious Triumph and much more victorious
Than Swords of words

To be together
As it shalt be forever
That is a delight for all of US
To be ONE
As only ONE
Unbound as free
As in solitude

Forever Thine
Forever Mine
Forever Ours

Jerusalem

Jerusalem,
The Temple Of Triumph
The Temple Of Eternity
The Temple Of Abiding
Begotten Sanctuary Of LOVE
Our Spirited Mother Of LOVE
Our glorious enduring
Queen of sacred heart
Jerusalem,
The Immortal Spiritual plane
Of mastery, purity and peace
Thy opulence tender majesty
Riveting as the begotten
First sacred word of universe
As sublime eternal treasure
to surmise, crowned with
grace and gallantry
As boundless Beloved
Queen of royalty
As rapturous eternal

Formidable flame of LOVE
Jerusalem,
Our Immortal Beloved,
Our LOVE rests on thy Beloved
Heart , utterly it is an endless
Ocean of devotion
With nay beginning or end

Jerusalem
Our Immortal Beloved Daughter of Zion
Our silk weaving Majestic Queen
from which all the garment
of LOVE and honor cometh
the splendid attire of King
Jerusalem,
Our Immortal Spiritual Consciousness
Thou art the seed of the tree of life
As Thy children as one nation
clinged to the tree of life
Shalt reign still,
as serving the majesty
of Heaven's Kingdom

Jerusalem,
Our Spirited Mother Of LOVE
We worship thy grace
of being in pure adoration
We long to embrace Thy Divine
Walls as embracing the
Fortitude Of LOVE
As children are weary
to dissipate and abscond

longing to touch the adoring
praising hands of their beloved mother,
O Jerusalem , the root of my being
Caressing our longing hands
As we art thy Loving Children Of Israel
And we shalt promise;
We wilt NOT cease from mortal
arbitrament NOR shall our swords
catch but a wink in our hands, as
We art hither beside thou to protect thou
We LOVE thou so dearly, O Jerusalem

Jerusalem,
Immortal Lion Of Judah,
Eternity jubilates Jerusalem as still
as an ineffable abided of Zion
Ruminating desire's elation
With an eternal roar of merriment
The effulgence of Thy glorious legacy
Vivified every sense of our being
As the children of Israel cherished
with pride to sow the seeds of wisdom
Conjoined in the petals of Thy past
bewildered by the endurance
and magnificence of Thy fortitude
O Jerusalem, let us rejoice and give
Songs of praise as the spirit of
Jerusalem ascends in delight jubilation
Heareth O Jerusalem, GOD
The Holy One Bless Be He;
is our Lord GOD, as His Benevolent candle
is unutterable, ineffably the Man's soul

Jerusalem,
The Immortal Champion Of Endurance
The tales of tranquility translucent
As the Devine source of all authority
At which hour we recite the Beloved
Name in the Book Of LOVE
Thy sacred pilgrimage holy site
Hath been the barrage of provocation,
Oh sweet bitterness,
The sheer immensity of Thy being
Wast did challenge twice
As the dust of The Temple Of LOVE
Did enter the hole of most wondrous
abyss drive to descend to the ordinary

O Jerusalem,
Yet Thy unfathomable grace
NEVER did disappear and our attributes
kindled the valley of begotten LOVE
Story and anon as Queen of our heart
Steered our Nation through tempest
Supernal beacons of light
Veil for infinite oneness
aspire the rhythms drifting
in the serenity of LOVE
As the Divine source of all authority

O precious Jerusalem,
Thy Majestic being is marry
the final revelation of Divine light,
thoughts, speech and deed
Unequivocally, Thou art the heart

Of Our Beloved ISRAEL,
The center of our ordinary,
The CAPITAL to exercise,
Authority and Kingship
And Thy magnificence walls,
As the blissful spiritual treasure
As the sacred eternal veils
Intoxicated with LOVE
As gentle bearing of Queen's hands
As the very embodiment of LOVE
As benevolent hands of Mother
of tenderness, as the fortitude Of LOVE
to shelter the heart of Elysium
As Jerusalem hath kept its
sacred embodiment of all secrets
As LOVE is concealed in the Holy Of Holies
the promise of Solomon as the Loving King
in his ample chair filling all eternity
Our Immortal Beloved JERUSALEM
Our Immortal Spirited Mother Of LOVE
Our Only Sacred Temple Of Triumph
We beseech Thou as Thy leigeman
Grant us to strive for Thy Glory
Grant us to strive for our eternal
Capital of our Gallant Nation Of ISRAEL
We Children Of ISRAEL stand in harmony
With our legions as warriors
to serve Thou to shield Thy presence
We shalt promise Thou to shield Thy presence
And nay hostile foes shalt ever invade
Thy Beloved Land as we Promise
TO NEVER EVER SEPARATE FROM THOU

As We art hither beside thou to protect THOU
We LOVE Thou So Dearly, O Jerusalem
We pray in harmony and LOVE
As our forefathers did pray
with silent passion longing to see
Thy visage for one gesture
Just for one more glance with thousand eyes
As the wings of their Emunah were
fluttered in merciful mirage to melt in bliss
Our Beloved Jerusalem Of Gold
Our Eternal Princess among provinces
The Immortal Spiritual plane
Of mastery, purity and peace
Thy opulence tender majesty
Riveting as the begotten
First sacred word of universe
As sublime eternal treasure to surmise
crowned with grace and gallantry
As boundless Beloved Queen of royalty
As rapturous eternal
Formidable flame Of LOVE

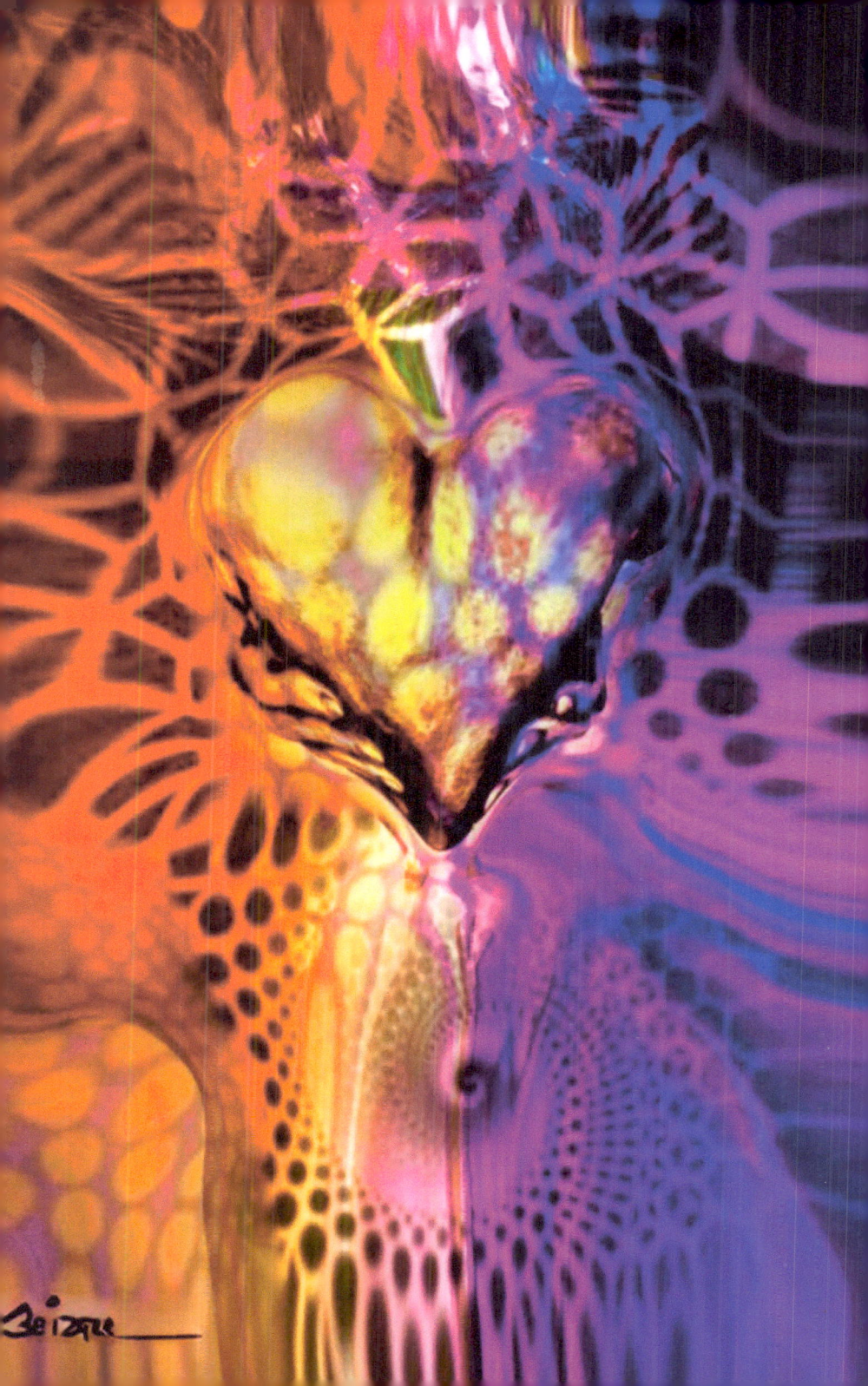

The Prayers

Adonai,
The Holy One Blessed Be He
Let us be the melting candle
of your beloved majesty
Our prayers have fevers to quell
As dancing in ecstasy of your beloved name
Your Beloved Name shines
in the Temple Of LOVE
As gentler passion slides into our hearts
As melting passionate candle
Embracing every word of
Your LOVE Story in pure jubilation

Your Temple Of Kindness bears
the art to kindle fierce desire as
the dearest LOVE Poems
Flaunting as purist innocence, sublime
silk of Devine music reciting
Your Beloved Benevolent
whisper of eternal LOVE

The Heavens lips ebb and flow
On Your endless ocean of LOVE
As the universe is in praise
living in eternity under the shadow of LOVE
circling in your Beloved kisses

The wheels of our heart beats
Your Loving name in harmony
As the parasol of LOVE prayers
brushes with the wings of ecstasy
to witness your explicit unequivocal LOVE
to bestow your supreme beloved
LOVE poems oeuvres of creation

FACE OF LOVE

This shalt be my allegorical
Poem to the ordinary of LOVE
If 't be true the voice wilt not
Carryeth the tongue then this
Epic Poem wilt giveth 't a pinion
As the wings of LOVE shalt
Carryeth the fragment of mine
Spirit as I unfold 't to thy wilt
At which hour in the point of
Thy Heart deep beneath
feigning effervescence,
Thy Beloved Heart's candle
blinks in melody, as the limpid
Truth Hymn Of LOVE arrives
at the sanctuary of gentleness
to wear the blanket of tenderness,
Thy Beloved Heart is face to face
with the majesty of LOVE
At which hour Thy Beloved Heart's
tears of immortal wounds bleeds LOVE

to nourish to heal the Seeds Of LOVE
Thy Beloved Heart is visage to visage
with the Majesty Of LOVE
At which hour the ordinary of compassion
Poured light into the cuppeth of Thy Heart
As the anointed Eyes of LOVE hast
reached the point of Thy Heart
As shields the swords Of awareness
as the fortitude of kindness
To bless every reason of Thy being, as
Thy Beloved Heart is face to face
with the Majesty Of LOVE
At which hour LOVE's Benevolent
touch did sew up all Thy tears of sorrow
with the needle of tenderness
and the thread of compassion
As the Divine LOVE milky sheen
of pearls hast embraced
Thy Beloved Heart in sublime jubilation
Thou art utterly visage to visage
As the face Of LOVE reflecting its
effulgence Majesty in Thy Beloved Heart

LOVE is a sublime riddle wrapped
in tenderness imbued with the
ardor kiss of Divinity sealed
in the Beloved relic of Thy Heart

Oh LOVE,
Thy benevolent mystical presence
Shalt lift its veil from the resplendence
Grandeur cosmic talismanic significance

As accorded confined fervent cognizance
As the flames of thousand candles
Glows a lambent light melting its
Heart in sublimity of the Majestic elegance
In an acme of perfection,
Welcoming the tender Heart burning
Wick of LOVE's word in exaltedness
Nobleness whence the Majestic
name of sublime LOVE is sealed
in The Temple Of LOVE in jubilation
Whence the souls brimful Of LOVE
dwells in the Infinite wisdom
As pure effulgence resplendence
Lights with gales of smiles glinting
of the Heart's Sea Of LOVE

Oh Loving Souls,
Embrace the LOVE of Humanity
Without any encumbrance
As an invincible Pious chronicle of life
that transcends all Hearts
As the gallant brave Sea Of LOVE
holds the foam of the Divinity
Oh Loving Souls;
The Trumpet Of Heroic Deeds,
Beware that Thy Loving Soul is
As incontrovertible and unequivocal
palmy intense luminous Orb Of Flame
With Passion Of Divinity
Oh Loving Souls,
The Trumpet Of Triumphal Joy;
Thy Loving Soul shalt NOT covet

Aught except respect to HUMANITY,
Compassion and wilt to HELP OTHERS
And let us brace ourselves to our Heart's
duties to be a Loving soul of value
to mete out justice whence souls
brimful Of LOVE shalt carryeth
the sublime torch of UNITY

As the beacon of excellence to guide
HUMANKIND to reconcile justice,
Liberty and Equality to woven the web
of SISTERHOOD and BROTHERHOOD
As all Souls shalt walk together
with vigor and ingenuity and shalt
Be side by side as ONE fabric of heart
Under the mere shadow UNITY of
Peace, LOVE and Majesty of Justice

As The Imperium Of Humanity shalt
Abide The Empire Of Hearts
As LOVE is the Divine elegance and beauty
of uniting by point by point mapping
the power of the congruence that transcends
one from achievement and fulfillment
to attainment and enlightenment

Oh Loving Hearts;
LOVE embodied the Infinite
compassion of Heart and the
Wisdom of Just that Soweth virtue
and valor of Souls in peerless
inherent tenderness and perfection

Oh Loving Abiding Hearts;
The Voyage Of Longing Hearts
Carries the basket of LOVE Poems
Songs in the cradle Of LOVE
Ensconced in pure utter contentment
As fervent blanket of Peace
As Thy Loving Soul is riding
On the Magic Carpet Of LOVE
Upon the scarlet sunset of Heart

Oh Loving Enduring Hearts;
Hearken to the Heartbeat Of Heart's
Sanctuary and Heareth the Sea Of LOVE
And sing the song of Thy silence
As Thy Beloved lips art silent ,
Unfettered by the bounds of reality, As
Thy Beloved Heart hath thousand tongues
Hearken to the Heroic Hymns Of Heart's
Haven and BREAKETH
THY OYSTER SHELL OF SILENCE
AS LOVE SHALT RISE IN ITS EFFULGENCE
LIMPID PURE TENDERNESS
TO QUENCH THE SPIRIT OF THY MIND
AS THE FERVENT SUBLIME OYSTER
OF THY BELOVED SOUL SHALT SUBMERGE
IN THE DEPTH OF ATTAINMENT
IN THE OCEAN OF DIVINE LOVE
TO RESCUE PURE HEARTS
TO FORM A BLISSED
PEARL OF DIVINE UNITY

And anon Thou hast arrived
TO THE POINT HEART
To see and witness THE VISAGE OF LOVE

As GOD, THE HOLY ONE, BLESSED BE HE
IS THE SUPREME BELOVED
EMBODIMENT OF ETERNAL LOVE
AS THE ULTIMATE POEM IS GOD
AS THOU ART LOVE
AS LOVE IS GOD
AS GOD IS LOVE
AS THE ULTIMATE POETRY IS LOVE

www.ingramcontent.com/pod-product-compliance
Lightning Source LLC
Chambersburg PA
CBHW042312150426
43199CB00001B/6